17.⁰⁰

DATE DUE

GAYLORD 234   PRINTED IN U. S. A.

974.9   12106   T07-315
S

Stewart, Mark.

New Jersey native peoples.

DEMCO

HEINEMANN STATE STUDIES

New Jersey
Native Peoples

Mark Stewart

Heinemann Library
Chicago, Illinois

© 2004 Heinemann Library
a division of Reed Elsevier Inc.
Chicago, Illinois

Customer Service 888-454-2279

Visit our website at www.heinemannlibrary.com

Designed by Heinemann Library
Page layout by Wilkinson Design
Printed and bound in the United States by
  Lake Book Manufacturing, Inc.

08 07 06 05 04
10 9 8 7 6 5 4 3 2 1

**Library of Congress
Cataloging-in-Publication Data**

Stewart, Mark, 1960-
  New Jersey Native peoples / Mark Stewart.
    p. cm. -- (State studies)
Summary: Provides an overview of New Jersey's
Native American peoples, including their history,
culture, government, and religion and their
life in Jew Jersey today.
Includes bibliographical references and index.
  ISBN 1-4034-0674-X (lib bdg.) --
ISBN 1-4034-2684-8 (pbk.)
 1. Indians of North America--New Jersey--History-
-Juvenile literature.
2. Indians of North America--New Jersey--Social
life and customs--Juvenile literature. [1. Indians of
North America--New Jersey.] I. Title. II. Series.
  E78.N6S82 2003
  974.9004'97--dc21

                                2003009428

Acknowledgments

The author and publishers are grateful to the
following for permission to reproduce copyright
material:

Cover photographs by (main) Bettmann/Corbis;
(row, L-R) Hulton Archive/Getty Images, John Kraft,
John Kraft, Bettmann/Corbis

Title page (L-R) North Wind Picture Archives,
The Nelson-Atkins Museum of Art/Kansas City,
Missouri, The Granger Collection, New York;
contents page, pp. 8, 18, 22, 23, 28, 29, 30, 32,
34 Robert Griffin/Bergen Historic Books; pp. 5, 6,
12, 33t John Kraft; pp. 11, 20 North Wind Picture
Archives; pp. 14, 25, 27, 38 Courtesy of the
New Jersey State Museum; p. 15 The Granger
Collection, New York; pp. 24, 37, 41 Marilyn
"Angel" Wynn/Native Stock; p. 26 Judd Pilossof/
FoodPix; p. 33b Jeff Zelevansky/AP Wide World
Photos; p. 36 The Nelson-Atkins Museum of
Art/Kansas City, Missouri; p. 43 Walt Marz

Photo research by John Klein

Special thanks to expert reader Chad Leinaweaver,
the Director for the Library at The New Jersey
Historical Society, for his help in the preparation
of this book.

Cover Pictures

Top (left to right) *Chief Lappawinze of
the Lenape, a wampum belt, a Lenape in
ceremonial dress, and an engraving of Henry
Hudson descending the Hudson River
around 1600.*
Main *Henry Hudson and party coming ashore
to meet the native people.*

Some words are shown in bold, **like this.**
You can find out what they mean by looking
in the glossary.

Contents

Early People

The first people came to North America thousands of years ago. These people entered the region during the last **Ice Age.** At that time, **glaciers** covered much of North America. Since more of the earth's water was frozen as ice, water levels were lower. A land bridge was exposed, stretching across the Bering Strait and connecting Asia with Alaska.

*Most American Indians believe their people have always been in the Americas. But most scientists think **prehistoric** Indians probably came from Asia, across the Bering Sea land bridge.*

Migration Routes

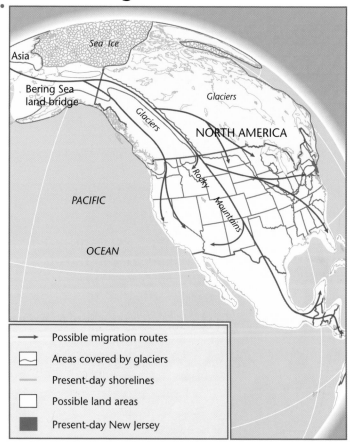

→	Possible migration routes
	Areas covered by glaciers
	Present-day shorelines
	Possible land areas
	Present-day New Jersey

4

Prehistoric hunters probably followed large animals, like the extinct mastodon, into the New Jersey region. The mastodon was similar to an elephant, with shaggy hair and long tusks.

PALEO-INDIANS

Most scientists believe that people known as Paleo-Indians began to **migrate** across the Bering Sea land bridge from Asia into North America about 30,000 years ago. Groups of these people eventually reached what is now New Jersey about 12,000 years ago. **Archaeologists** have studied stone tools, weapons, and other **artifacts** found along the Delaware River in Sussex County. Based on these findings, they believe that bands of Paleo-Indian hunter-gatherers followed large **game animals** into the region.

ARCHAIC INDIANS

The Archaic period started when the climate became warmer around 8000 **B.C.E.** By that time, plants had changed and many large animals once hunted by Paleo-Indians had become **extinct.** Indians of the Archaic

New Jersey's Native Peoples

PALEO-INDIANS	ARCHAIC	WOODLAND	HISTORIC INDIANS
ca. 10,000 B.C.E. to 8000 B.C.E.	ca. 8000 B.C.E. to 1000 B.C.E.	ca. 1000 B.C.E. to 1500 C.E.	ca. 1500 C.E. to Present

*A New Jersey Lenape named Lone Bear is pictured here in **traditional** dress. Lenape men wore shirts, **breechcloths,** leggings, and moccasins, all made from deerskin.*

period hunted deer, elk, bear, and moose. They also ate fish and shellfish. Toward the end of the Archaic period, Indians may have raised food in small gardens. Archaic Indians also made stone tools and carved bowls from rock.

WOODLAND INDIANS

The Woodland period begins around 1000 **B.C.E.** The first settlements in New Jersey in this period were probably in the highlands north of the Raritan River. There is evidence that Woodland Indians used the natural rock shelters there as base camps for their activities. We also know that these early people of New Jersey took full advantage of the abundant food supply in its rivers and lakes. They fished in the Raritan, Passaic, Delaware, and Hudson Rivers, and also collected crawfish and freshwater **mussels.** Around 1,000 years ago, Woodland Indians began to farm the land for the first time.

HISTORIC INDIANS

The **prehistoric** people of New Jersey were the **ancestors** of the American Indians who lived in the state when the first white people arrived in the 1500s. Those Indians of the 1500s called themselves *Lenape* (len-AH-pay), which means "original people." Europeans called them the Delaware Indians, because they lived near the Delaware River.

The Lenape

The Lenape were a part of the Algonquian language group. Their nations stretched up and down the Atlantic coast. Because of their reputation for being fair and just, Lenape leaders were often called upon to settle disputes among other Algonquian tribes.

Right before the first Europeans arrived in the 1500s, the Lenape **culture** changed. The New Jersey Indians

Lenape Territory in New Jersey

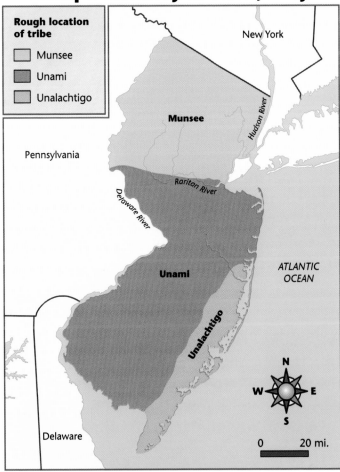

Rough location of tribe
- ☐ Munsee
- ■ Unami
- ☐ Unalachtigo

New York

Pennsylvania

Munsee

Hudson River

Rariton River

Delaware River

Unami

ATLANTIC OCEAN

Unalachtigo

Delaware

N W E S

0   20 mi.

This map shows the rough territories of the three Lenape groups of New Jersey around 1600. In daily life, each Lenape village really governed itself, despite being part of a larger group.

When the Lenape first saw Giovanni da Verrazano's ship on the horizon in 1524, they could not have known the terrible effects Europeans would ultimately have on their people.

began mixing with the people of the Nanticoke River in Southeastern Delaware and the Eastern Shore of Maryland (the Tidewater People), who were **migrating** north. They blended into Lenape society, increasing the population from a few thousand to perhaps as many as 12,000 or more.

THREE GROUPS

The New Jersey Lenape spoke three distinct but related languages. Those living roughly north of the Raritan River spoke Munsee. They were known as the people of the stony country. In the south were the Unami Lenape, known as the people down the river. A third group, called the Unalachtigo Lenape, lived along the Atlantic coast. Unalachtigo translated means "The People Who Live by the Ocean." Among these three groups, almost all the land that is present-day New Jersey was under Lenape control and was known as *Lenapehoking*, or "Land of the Lenape."

MEETING THE EUROPEANS

The native people of New Jersey saw the first white people in 1524, when Italian explorer Giovanni da Verrazano, working for France, sailed up the Atlantic coast past several Lenape settlements. Verrazano wrote of native people who came aboard his ship, and these are believed to be Lenape. Another face-to-face meeting occurred in 1609, when English sea captain Henry Hudson anchored his ship, the *Half Moon*, in Sandy Hook Bay. The sailors went ashore in search of freshwater and food, and the curious and friendly Lenape met them, eager to trade. According to a journal later published by one of Hudson's men, disagreements broke out between the sailors and the Lenape, and the *Half Moon* later sailed away.

The first Europeans to really explore New Jersey were Dutch traders, who established trading posts in southern New York during the 1620s. They were followed by Swedish, French, and English adventurers. With few exceptions, these white people had no regard for the rights and territories of the Lenape. They hunted and trapped where they wanted, when they wanted, and set up camps in places the Lenape had been using for generations.

TRADE

At first, the Lenape put up with the Europeans. The Europeans had trade items the Lenape had never seen before, and they were willing to swap them for animal

Fighting with the Dutch

When New Jersey was under Dutch rule, there were many conflicts between American Indians and the white settlers. In 1643, a group of soldiers **ambushed** a Lenape camp in Pavonia (now Jersey City and Hoboken) and spared no one. They killed 80 people, including women and children. This act so outraged the native people in the region that the Iroquois (who were anything but friendly neighbors to the Lenape) and other tribes took revenge by launching attacks on New York's Dutch settlers. It took two years for the fighting to stop.

Even after the English took over the New Jersey colony, tension between Dutch settlers and the Lenape always seemed very high. In 1650, a Lenape girl was picking peaches on the property of a Dutchman, who became angry and killed her. This began the "Peach War," which saw more brutality and violence, especially in northern New Jersey.

pelts, particularly beaver. The Lenape were expert trappers, so trade in the early years was active. The Europeans traded everything from metal farming tools to brightly colored cloth. The Lenape were especially interested in glass beads, which they often used to decorate clothing.

What at first seemed like a good idea to the native people of New Jersey turned out to be a very bad one. Trading with the Europeans turned Lenape life upside

down. For hundreds of years, the Lenape hunted animals for food and clothing. The Lenape took only what they needed, so the animal populations they hunted had a chance to recover. But the balance was upset when they began hunting more animals than they needed, so they could have extra pelts to trade. In a short time, the numbers of the animals the Lenape hunted for food greatly decreased.

These Lenape are bringing beaver skins to trade with white men. The European demand for beaver skins caused the Lenape to kill more of the animals than they needed for the first time in their history.

DISEASE

The worst effect on the Lenape of contact with the Europeans was the diseases that the Europeans brought

*Lenape **medicine men** treated the sick and wounded with **herbs** and traditional methods. The child on the left is in a sweat lodge trying to sweat the sickness out of the body. The Lenape had no resistance or treatments for European diseases, and thousands died as a result.*

across the Atlantic Ocean. The Lenape had no **immunity** to the diseases they caught from their European trading partners. And because the **traditional** Lenape way of treating the sick was to gather the family around them, the spread of illnesses such as **smallpox** and **measles** could not be stopped. Every few years, an **epidemic** would sweep through the Lenape population, killing thousands. By 1700, less than 100 years after the first European colonists set foot in New Jersey, the Indian population in the colony had decreased from about 12,000 to only about 2,400 to 3,000.

LOSS OF LAND

With Lenape life more and more dependent on trade with the settlers, and the native populations dropping fast, there was nothing to stop the European colonists from taking all the Lenape's land. The American Indians of New Jersey were puzzled by the colonists' ideas of land ownership. The Lenape did not believe that land could be owned. They believed that the earth was a living thing that would outlast any human, so in their view everyone had a right to use it. As a result, the

Just Making A Living

As the Lenape nation went into steep decline and its villages disappeared, many of those who stayed in New Jersey had to find work. Some took jobs with the European settlers as servants or farmhands. Others became scouts for the British. A few decided to work for the French, who were the enemy of the British. Those who felt more comfortable living with other American Indians chose to work for the Iroquois. Many Lenape left their land forever, joining the crews of merchant ships and whaling ships.

Lenape mistakenly signed treaties and accepted goods in return for giving land to the settlers.

When the Lenape finally realized that the Europeans did not share their belief about land ownership, they fought to get their land back. There were many violent conflicts with Dutch settlers, who considered the American Indians little more than pests. The Dutch had so little regard for New Jersey's native people that they even considered the possibility of making them slaves. After the English took over the New Jersey colony from the Dutch in 1655, Lenape **diplomats** learned how the English court system worked. They began to challenge the legality of the documents they signed that gave the land to the European settlers. Sometimes this action worked, and sometimes it did not.

In 1658, the English signed a treaty with the Iroquois and many other American Indian groups in the northeastern

United States. The Lenape had no choice but to join in the treaty. In the years that followed, Iroquois people took over land in northern New Jersey and claimed authority over all the Lenape people. The Iroquois disliked their southern neighbors, believing them to be weak and foolish. They treated the Lenape very cruelly. Meanwhile, European settlers pushed inland from the coast. Too weak to resist both groups, the Lenape nation began to break apart. Some Lenape converted to **Christianity** and tried to become part of the new European **culture.** Others left New Jersey for settlements in Pennsylvania, Ohio, and Canada.

THE DECLINE OF THE LENAPE

The few Lenape who stayed in New Jersey were treated harshly. In Delaware, there was a Lenape uprising against the colonists that spilled into parts of New Jersey. British soldiers put down the revolt. By the 1750s, the Lenape had lost all their land.

*The experiment of the Brotherton **Reservation** failed after only 44 years. The remaining Lenape moved to New York in 1802 to live with Iroquoian Indians. This illustration shows the Lenape preparing to move from Brotherton.*

In 1758, the New Jersey Assembly voted to give the remaining Lenape, at this point just about 200, a small piece of land in present-day Burlington County. This was the first Indian reservation in New Jersey. A **Presbyterian** minister named John Brainerd was sent to oversee the reservation, which he called Brotherton.

Safe Haven?

As the Lenape were being overrun by white settlers, some looked for protection among the Moravians. This branch of Christianity preached sharing and nonviolence. Moravians founded many New Jersey towns, including Hope, Shrewsbury, and Middletown. Hundreds of Lenape converted to Christianity in these areas.

In the 1760s, an Ottawa chief named Pontiac (pictured at left, addressing a council) led an uprising against the British in what is today Detroit, Michigan. When this revolt was stopped, many colonists targeted peaceful Moravian Lenape for revenge. Being nonviolent, the Lenape chose not to fight back, and were massacred in large numbers while praying and singing hymns.

Brainerd hoped to get the Lenape people back on their feet by teaching job skills and preaching religion. He helped the Lenape set up a sawmill and **gristmill** in what is now known as Indian Mills.

For almost twenty years, life in Brotherton was bearable for the Lenape. But when Brainerd became ill in 1777 and left the **reservation,** it went into sharp decline. The

Last Lenape of New Jersey

One of the Lenape that stayed in southern New Jersey after the Brotherton reservation was abandoned was known to all as "Indian Ann." Born in 1805, she was the daughter of Lashar Tamar, the last chief of the Lenape. During the 1800s, she scratched out a living making straw baskets for local residents and tourists. She preferred to trade her baskets rather than sell them. This made her an important part of the community. When people baked an extra pie or butchered a hog, they would set the extra aside to trade for Indian Ann's baskets.

Indian Ann was married twice, first to a former slave and then to an African-American freeman. She raised seven children near Indian Mills. Her second husband, John Roberts, fought and died in the Civil War (1861–1865) with the famous 22nd Regiment of African-American troops. After the war, Indian Ann lived off the **pension** due to her husband, but she continued to make baskets. She was impossible to miss, loaded down with baskets and smoking a long clay pipe as she ambled back and forth on the road connecting Vincetown and Mt. Holly. Indian Ann died in 1894, and as far as anyone knows, she was the last full-blooded Lenape to live her entire life in New Jersey. Her grave, in the Methodist Cemetery in Tabernacle, is now an official historic site.

American Revolution had started in 1775 and was still being fought. The Lenape were all but forgotten by both the British and the American colonists. The Lenape lived in **poverty** until the Mahican, another Algonquian group, suggested they leave New Jersey and live with them near Oneida Lake in **upstate** New York. The New Jersey **legislature** agreed to sell the land in Burlington County and give part of the money to the remaining Lenape, who now numbered only about 85 people, for their move to New York.

In May of 1802, Lashar Tamar, the last Lenape chief at Brotherton, led his people to New Stockbridge, New York. A handful of Lenape stayed behind and blended into the surrounding southern New Jersey communities. Others moved north and settled in northern New Jersey and Pennsylvania. Chief Tamar himself eventually returned to southern New Jersey and settled on a farm near the town of Rancocas.

The New Jersey Lenape lived among the Mahican in New York until 1832. Hoping to make a new home at that time, they asked for the rest of the money from the Brotherton Reservation sale. The New Jersey Legislature awarded them $2,000. With only 40 members left, the Lenape resettled with American Indian groups west of the Mississippi River and in Canada.

OKLAHOMA LENAPE

A group of Lenape eventually moved into Texas, where they lived with Caddo Indians. Like most American Indians, these Lenape were forced into Indian Territory in present-day Oklahoma in the 1800s. In 1859, they settled in Anadarko, Oklahoma. Today, this is the only Lenape community in the United States that is recognized by the United States government.

Lenape Life and Organization

Lenape **culture** centered around the **clan.** This was an extended family group that helped people identify themselves as being related, much like a person's last name does today. In fact, when the Lenape encountered other Lenape whom they did not know, they would often give their clan name before their own.

LENAPE TRIBES AND CLANS

There were three major tribes among the New Jersey Lenape. In the northern part of the state lived the Munsees. They tended to live in large groups, near lakes and rivers. In the central and southern regions were the Unami. Their villages were smaller and more spread out. In the southern part of New Jersey, along the coast, were the Unalachtigo. The three main clans found within all three Lenape tribes were the Wolf, Turtle, and Turkey clans. Throughout the region, there were also about twenty other less important clans.

Lenape clans were like large, extended families. They were **matrilineal,** which means membership was traced through

This is a Lenape knot bowl. Making pottery for cooking and storage was part of the work Lenape women performed.

the mother. Young women were not allowed to marry within their own clan, which meant their husbands had to join their clan after marriage. This made it unlikely for one clan to do something bad to another, because there were almost always members in each clan who were closely related to members of other clans.

WORK

The Lenape divided work among men, women, children, and the elderly. As a rule, men hunted and fished. Women planted and harvested crops; gathered wild nuts, roots, and berries; and prepared meals. With the Lenape, however, the roles of men and women were not as strictly divided as with some other American Indian tribes. Children were the responsibility of the

Marriage

The Lenape were unusual because they did not arrange marriages for their young people. Although council **elders** had to approve of a couple before they wed, they let young people decide for themselves who would make the best husbands and wives. The courting process was very formal, but romantic as well. The men delivered secret messages to the women they hoped to marry, and sang **ritual** songs to them. The marriage **ceremony** was fairly simple. Once a couple received approval for their marriage, the man presented his future wife with a piece of meat to show he was a good hunter, and she cooked it to show she was a good wife. They shared a meal together and then left for a short hunting trip, much like today's honeymoon.

Lenape men sometimes helped the women harvest corn and other crops. In many other tribes, women did the farming by themselves.

elders. Clan elders taught children Lenape **traditions** and the basics of village life, often through storytelling.

Lenape children helped the women of the tribe gather food. Gathered food was a large part of the Lenape diet. Foods gathered from the region included persimmons, grapes, beach plums, huckleberries, cranberries, strawberries, blackberries, walnuts, hickory nuts, roots, and **herbs.** The Lenape also harvested wild honey. Lenape women wove baskets from grass and thin strips of wood and bark. They used these baskets to carry the gathered food.

Cooking Pots

The pots in which the Lenape cooked stews were made by rolling clay into long, thin strips, then coiling the pieces into the desired shape. The wet pot was then pressed into a mold dug into the earth and buried until it hardened.

Lenape girls learned everything from how to make pots and baskets to how to sew clothes. Boys learned how to track **game animals** and catch fish, how to build **wigwams,** how to trade, and even how to defend the village against attack. Lenape children were taught to be tough. Mothers dunked their babies in cold streams every day to toughen them up. Cold water was also used to scold naughty children who misbehaved. The Lenape never hit their children however.

The Lenape were unusual among American Indians, because jobs were sometimes shared or interchanged. Young men and women were expected to fulfill their traditional roles, but as they grew older it was not unusual for them to perform other duties. Men might be asked to help with the gathering or preparation of food,

Lenape Names

There were no doctors or hospitals as we know them in Lenape society, so when children became seriously ill, they often died. For this reason, babies were not given names when they were born. Instead, they were given nicknames. Only after they reached the age of five did a Lenape child receive a real name, and this came from a special tribal name-giver. This name was **sacred** and was known only to its owner, the spirits, and the name-giver. Everyone else continued to use the person's nickname.

and there is evidence that women sometimes participated in battle. The role of the **medicine man** was not exclusively male, either. The Lenape believed that anyone who possessed special healing powers or a great spiritual gift, determined through dreams or visions, could be a medicine man or woman.

THE IMPORTANCE OF SEASONS

The changing seasons were important to the everyday life of the Lenape. In the spring, a Lenape village would pack up and move to a lake or river swelled by the winter thaw. In the summer came another move, this time to the coast, where shellfish could be collected and fish could be caught. The Lenape used hooks made of bone in deep water and **harpoons** and arrows in the shallow waters. A good summer spot also had to have rich soil, so

Every fall, larger Lenape villages held a **ceremony** *called the* Gam'wing *in their Big Houses, as shown here. A chosen Lenape would use a series of sticks with symbols to chant the tribe's history and story of creation. The* Gam'wing *also gave thanks for the harvest and called on the spirits for a successful hunt.*

crops such as corn, beans, and squash could be planted.

Summer was a favorite season. The Lenape were extremely comfortable on and in the water. They traveled along rivers and lakes in canoes. They were also tremendous swimmers, and could hold their breath underwater for a very long time. Summer was also a good time for trading with the different **clans** and the villages located along the long stretch of the Atlantic coast.

The Lenape used dugout canoes for travel, fishing, and trading between villages. Travel by water was the fastest and easiest way to go at that time, unless there was too much ice during the winter months.

In the late summer and fall, the members of a Lenape village would harvest their crops and prepare for winter by drying them, along with meat and other foods. The Lenape stored these items in cool, dry places once they reached their winter camps. They stored them in overhead racks inside the **wigwam,** or in pits lined with tree bark. As the weather grew cooler in fall, the Lenape would form large hunting parties. They were very good at killing deer, bears, and turkeys with spears or bows and arrows. Sometimes they would set small fires to drive all of the large animals into a narrow area, where they could be hunted in large numbers more easily.

Hunting continued into the winter, as large animals moved more slowly and were easy to track in the snow. But after

Lenape Clothing

The Lenape wardrobe was not unlike that of other Algonquian people. Men and boys wore **breechcloths** during warm weather, adding deerskin leggings and robes made of fur and feathers during the winter. Women and girls wore deerskin dresses when it was warm, and leggings and fur in the colder months. All Lenapes wore moccasins on their feet.

a successful summer and fall, the Lenape mostly looked forward to spending time with family and friends. The winter months were a time for celebration, prayer, and planning. Clan members often gathered for huge feasts, and dressed in their finest **ceremonial** clothing. There was much singing and dancing. After a happy winter, the Lenape were ready to begin the cycle all over again.

THE TYPICAL LENAPE DAY

A normal day in a Lenape village began right after sunrise, with a filling breakfast. This was sometimes the only big meal until the following morning. The women would make a stew, which simmered over a fire all day. During the day, villagers could take what they wanted whenever they wanted. However, they usually gathered for a second meal in the late afternoon.

During the summer months, the Lenape traveled to the coast for shellfish. Mounds of shells can still be seen today along the New Jersey coast.

Unless a feast or ceremony was planned, the men usually left the village in search of food. At the same time, women and children went about the day-to-day chores that kept the village going. This included making food. Cornmeal was a main food. The Lenape also baked bread made from a soft, white corn called *po'hem*. They also prepared corn in many other ways.

Lenape men hunted alone or in groups. Sometimes the animals were followed for hours by hunters wearing animal disguises, as shown here. Often the animal was only wounded, and the hunter followed his prey until it became exhausted.

Succotash is a mixture of corn and beans. It was a popular food of the Lenape and is still eaten today.

Vegetables and grains were mixed and mashed in a *tahk-wa-ho'a-kan,* which is the hollowed-out log of a gum tree. There was a *tahk-wa-ho'a-kan* sitting outside almost every Lenape home. A favorite dish of the Lenape was a soup consisting of corn, beans, dried meat, and bear's grease. Beans and corn were cooked together to make succotash, a dish that is still eaten today. Pumpkin and squash were mashed and used in a variety of ways. The Lenape also ate strawberries, raspberries, onions, crabapples, and nuts, which grew in the region where they lived.

FUN TIME

Except during extreme weather conditions, the Lenape found they could collect and grow food fairly easily. This left time for fun and games. Boys wrestled, boxed, and practiced their hunting skills in contests. Among their favorite games were a kind of **rugby,** and a contest where spear-like poles were thrown through rolling hoops. This sharpened the skills they would need to hunt. Lenape girls did not usually participate in these physical activities. Instead they often made cornhusk dolls and learned the tasks they would later perform as women of the tribe.

The Lenape and Their Environment

Before the Europeans arrived in New Jersey, the Lenape depended completely on their **environment** for the things they needed to live. This meant moving from place to place during the year. To the Lenape, the moves were a part of life. As a result, a Lenape village was able to pick up and move at a moment's notice. Each family within a village

*During the hunting season at the end of summer and in early fall, parties of men often camped in natural caves and rock shelters. Most of the meat they obtained was **smoked** and taken home for later use.*

Waste Not, Want Not

When a Lenape hunter was fortunate enough to kill a large animal, he carried it back to the village, where every last scrap of the animal was put to use. The meat, liver, and heart were eaten, the skin was used to make clothing and other items, the animal's bones and teeth were used to make tools or ornaments, and anything that was left went into a pot to make a stew.

was responsible for all of its possessions, and had to be able to break down and set up a **wigwam** quickly and efficiently. Once established in a location, the people immediately began to adapt to the new **environment.**

USING THE FOREST

Though known for their skill on the water, the Lenape lived a good part of the year in a thickly forested environment. Oak, beech, hickory, ash, and chestnut trees filled the landscape. Near the mountain regions, white pines and hemlocks stretched high toward the sky. The Lenape depended on forests for almost everything. From the trees they cut down came materials for many everyday items, including tools, musical instruments, and weapons. From the land they cleared sprang the crops that made up most of their food. And from the forest animals they hunted

Longhouse

Some Lenape villages had longhouses, similar to those used by the Iroquois in New York. These buildings were about 50 feet long and housed several families. In all of these buildings, people sat and slept on wooden benches, not on the ground.

came the meat, bones, skins, and **sinew** they needed to survive.

Hickory and ash trees were perfect for making bows and arrows, while chestnut trees were often used for canoes. The forest also supplied the lumber needed to build a Big House. The high ceiling of the Big House was meant to represent the heavens. The floor, which was 100 feet or more across, represented the earth. A central post holding up the roof connected

Home Sweet Home

The word *wigwam* comes from the Algonquian word for "house." A wigwam was made by cutting down saplings (mostly ash trees) and arranging them in the ground in a circle. The tops were bent in toward the center and tied together. This was then strengthened with sticks lashed horizontally to this framework. This wooden frame was then covered with bark shingles or mats, which were held together with mud plaster and layered so that rain could not leak in. The floor was covered with animal hides. People slept on wooden benches arranged along the walls. Food was stored overhead on special racks, and other everyday items were placed on shelves built against the walls. The wigwam was a perfect house for the Lenape. When the time came to move their village, they could roll up their mats and skins and set up a new one in a matter of hours.

heaven and earth, which made the Big House a very special place. An oval drawn around this post was called the Great White Path, which is how the Lenape described the Milky Way. That was the place where all spirits were thought to live.

For a time, New Jersey's forests even offered the Lenape protection from the white settlers. Europeans were scared of going into the dark forest, and they usually stayed close to the water. At first, this seemed to work for the Lenape. They hunted animals for meat and fur and traded with white settlers for items they needed. Unfortunately, this contact with the Europeans brought about the deadly diseases that killed many Lenapes.

*This Lenape **medicine man** in a wolfskin headdress is using **herbs,** specific words and song, and a turtle shell rattle to cure a sick person lying on a bearskin rug.*

Lenape Advantage

During the time when the Dutch ruled New Jersey, they had many battles with the Lenape. The Dutch thought that a heavily armed, modern army would have no trouble getting rid of such a simple enemy. They were wrong.

The Lenape had lived in this land for hundreds of years and knew every inch of it by heart. Dutch officers, working without maps, constantly led their men into **ambushes.** After a while, the Dutch soldiers did not want to go into New Jersey's forests for fear of attack.

There was no way the forests could protect them from those diseases.

Before the Lenape caught European diseases, they were very successful in treating many illnesses. They counted on the forest for all of their medicines. They knew which plants and trees produced chemicals that could ease pain and slow infection. To reduce fevers, for example, the inner bark from dogwood trees was dried, ground into powder, and brewed into a tea.

USING THE WATER

New Jersey's waterways played an important part in Lenape life. They were the region's highways, moving people and goods from place to place by canoe. In the spring and fall, many Lenape villages moved to riverbanks, including those along the Delaware, Hackensack, Raritan, Passaic, and Musconetcong Rivers.

*Groups of Lenape took advantage of the large numbers of fish that **migrated** up New Jersey's rivers each spring to deposit their eggs.*

These bodies of water were filled with shad, salmon, herring, catfish, and sturgeon. The men constructed large nets, weighted with stones, which they stretched across large sections to capture many fish at once.

In the summer, the Lenape villages that were close enough would move to rivers and inlets near the Atlantic Ocean. These areas, where freshwater meets saltwater, were as rich with life then as they are today. The Lenape were experts when it came to the harvesting of shellfish, particularly oysters and clams. They used the leftover shells to make beautiful **ceremonial wampum** beads. In the 1600s, wampum belts were highly prized by European traders. A skillfully made wampum belt could be traded for many supplies.

USING THE SOIL

Like today's farmers, the native people of New Jersey found the soil to be very rich. The Lenape generally farmed at higher elevations, and avoided the state's low-lying areas. They chopped down patches of forest and sometimes burned the rough stumps to enrich the soil. After a few harvests, a field lost its nutrients and would no longer be used for planting. A new field would be created. The abandoned land attracted deer and

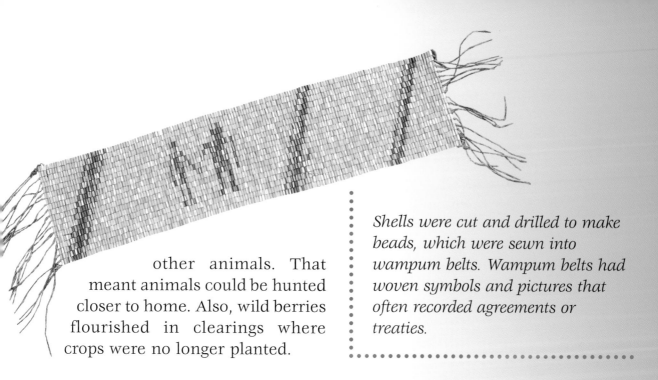

other animals. That meant animals could be hunted closer to home. Also, wild berries flourished in clearings where crops were no longer planted.

Shells were cut and drilled to make beads, which were sewn into wampum belts. Wampum belts had woven symbols and pictures that often recorded agreements or treaties.

In a typical Lenape village, women were responsible for tending the crops. Each spring they planted several varieties of corn, beans, squash, pumpkins, and tobacco. The Lenape did not plant in rows, like the white settlers. Lenape women planted each vegetable in easy spots between whatever tree stumps were left in the field. Corn, beans, and squash grew especially

When the Lenape abandoned a field after a few harvests, wild grasses grew in quickly. This attracted deer and other animals, which could then be hunted close to home.

well together and were known as the Three Sisters. Corn stalks helped to support the vines of the beans as they grew. The Lenape nourished the crops throughout the summer, protected them from animals and insects, and then harvested them in the fall.

Whatever was not eaten was preserved for the winter months. The Lenape developed some very effective ways of drying their crops for later use. Squash was cut into strips, while corn stalks and bean stems were braided and left to dry in the sun on racks. Dried kernels of corn were roasted over a fire and placed in clay pots, which could be stored for long periods of time in pits dug into the ground.

During the summer months, Lenape women took care of the crops with a crooked stick, chipped stone hoe, or the shoulder blade of a deer tied to a wooden shaft.

Lenape Beliefs

The Lenape were a very **spiritual** people. Like other American Indian groups, they felt they were one with nature. They believed the earth, its plants, and its creatures should be respected. The Lenape believed there were higher powers watching over them. They also believed that every living thing had a spirit, called a *manito.* Good spirits brought favorable weather and good luck, and bad spirits brought insect bites and illness.

THE CREATION

The Lenape traced their beginnings back to a creator named *Kishelemukong,* who brought up a giant turtle from the bottom of an endless ocean. The creature grew even bigger once it reached the water's surface. It grew so large, in fact, that its shell became the great stretch of land now known as North America. The Lenape believed that a tree sprouted in the middle of this huge territory. The first man was born from one of the tree's roots. He was then joined by a woman born from another root. *Kishelemukong* next created the sun, moon, and everything else the Lenape observed in the night sky. The creator was also responsible for all animals and plants, as well as the changing of the seasons.

OTHER SPIRITS

The four winds that blew over New Jersey during the different seasons were known to the Lenape as the "gambling grandparents." For example, when the cold winds from the north began to howl, the Lenape

Doll Dance

This is a Lenape *Ohta,* or Doll Being. The Lenape believed such Doll Beings had the power to protect their owner's health if they were given offerings and dances and treated well.

The power of *Ohtas* was said to be discovered after a lonely child made a cornhusk doll to serve as her dance partner. When it was realized the doll possessed life and understanding, Lenape people everywhere carved *Ohtas* from wood and joined in yearly Doll Dances to ask for good fortune and good health.

believed that "our grandfather where it is winter" was winning a game of chance. As spring began to bloom, they rejoiced that "our Grandmother where it is warm" was winning. Spring was the only season brought on by a woman.

The Lenape's relationship with their world included an interest in the sun, which they called "Elder Brother." He sat proudly in the sky wearing yellow face paint and a fiery headdress of red feathers. The moon was considered a brother, too. So were thunder and lightning. The Lenape thought that storms were visited upon them by "Thunder Beings," which were massive birds with human faces that launched lightning-bolt arrows.

The Lenape also honored the corn spirit, whom they called "Mother Corn." She blessed them with rich crops of corn, as well as beans, squash, and other plants. The Lenape prayed to this supernatural power and made sacrifices to her. For example, when men returned from a successful hunt, they frequently set aside the largest deer killed. Rather than eat it, they would offer it as a gift to the corn spirit. The yearly **ceremony** held for Mother Corn was called the Mask Dance. The main dish served was **hominy.** Held during the fall harvest, the Mask Dance was one of the most important times of the year for the Lenape. Other important Lenape events included a Green Corn celebration in the summer, as well as festivals held for the first fruits of summer and the fall harvest. During these celebrations, the Lenape feasted, danced, and showed their appreciation to the spirits.

The Lenape were excellent hunters and farmers, yet they believed spirits helped them in both areas. The spirit that guided hunters was known as "Living Solid Face." He gave direction to those lost in the wilderness and looked after deer, bear, and other big

This is a closeup of a Lenape mask that might have been used in the Mask Dance. Each mask was different. Sometimes hair was also attached to the top.

animals, always keeping them close to a Lenape village. The Lenape held a **ceremony** in the spirit's honor every year. They offered thanks for his powers and prayed for a successful hunting season. During the **ritual,** a man would dress in a bearskin robe and a red-and-black mask.

The Lenape believed their relationship with animals to be a **sacred** one. The story of *Nan'a-push* (also known as *A-men'a-push*), which is a slightly different version of the creation story, shows this relationship. *Nan'a-push* was a powerful being who lived on Earth during the time of a

The Lenape carved masks on living trees. That way the spirit of the forest would be contained in the mask. They would then cut the mask away from the tree and paint it, usually red and black.

great flood. He sought shelter on the highest mountain peak he could find. When *Nan'a-push* realized the waters were not going down, he gathered all the birds and other animals and shielded them in his robe. Eventually, *Nan'a-push* was forced to climb a large cedar tree to protect the animals and himself. He broke off limbs from the tree and built a huge raft. While floating on the water, *Nan'a-push* decided to create a new world, with the help of the creatures stranded with him. He sent one animal after another under water to get a piece of earth. When each came back, close to death, *Nan'a-push* breathed life back into them. The muskrat finally completed the task. *Nan'a-push* placed the handful of mud on the back of a turtle, and from there the earth grew again.

Vision Quest

The greatest Lenape ceremony of all was the *Gam'wing,* a yearly worship ritual held in the Big House. The *Gam'wing,* which lasted twelve days, included dances, songs, and other religious displays. The Lenape dressed in their finest clothes and prepared **elaborate** meals for this ceremony.

Participation in the *Gam'wing* marked a teenage boy's journey into adulthood. To take part, a Lenape teenager had to find his "vision," which was an outlook on life that captured his deepest feelings. This was done during a period of **fasting** in the forest called a "vision quest." Once the vision came, the young man had to make up a chant that explained his vision and perform it at the *Gam'wing.*

New Jersey Indians Today

More and more white settlers came to New Jersey in the 1700s and 1800s, pushing out the Lenape. The Unalachtigo left for New York state around 1725. The Munsee left around 1742. They settled in southeastern Pennsylvania, and later moved on to Ohio and Indiana. Some Munsees also moved into Canada, while others settled around the Kansas and Missouri Rivers. In 1867, many Lenapes moved to the Indian Territory in what is

Indian Reservations in New Jersey

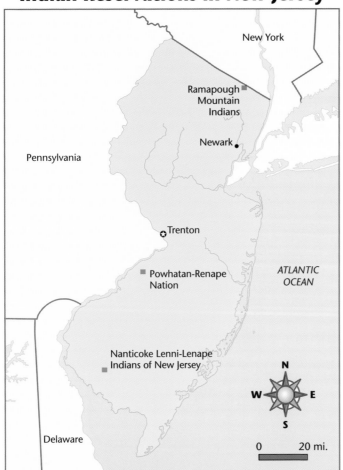

*Though they are not officially recognized by the federal government, there are three **reservations** in New Jersey, for its three state-recognized tribes.*

now Oklahoma. There they were **incorporated** into the Cherokee tribe. A few Lenape also went to Green Bay, Wisconsin.

NEW JERSEY TRIBES TODAY

In 2003, the State of New Jersey recognized three American Indian tribes. They are the Nanticoke Lenni-Lenape Indians, the Powhatan-Renape Nation, and the Ramapough Mountain Indians.

THE NANTICOKE LENNI-LENAPE INDIANS

The Nanticoke Lenni-Lenape Indians of New Jersey are the largest active tribe in the state and were recognized by the New Jersey state government in 1982. The tribe is made up of about 1,500 families. The Nanticoke people **migrated** north through New Jersey in the early 1600s. Through this migration they united with the Lenape Indians already living in New Jersey. The Nanticoke were also known as the Tidewater People.

Members of the Nanticoke Lenni-Lenape tribe work to preserve the tribe's **culture.** They do this by teaching **traditional** dancing, drumming, and the making of Indian crafts to people of all

This man is performing a traditional dance at the Nanticoke Lenni-Lenape Powwow.

ages. Every year the Nanticoke hold a powwow. Here they show and share the skills of the tribe's **heritage.**

The Nanticoke Lenni-Lenape Indians' headquarters are located in Bridgeton, New Jersey, in Cumberland County. The office assists tribal members with housing, food, jobs, education, and other necessities. The headquarters also keeps a history of the tribe.

THE POWHATAN-RENAPE NATION

This American Indian nation is located at the Rankokus Indian **Reservation** in Rancocas, New Jersey, in Burlington County. The Powhatan-Renape were recognized by the State of New Jersey in 1980. Members of this group work to provide services to American Indians. They also work to educate other people in New Jersey, especially the school children, about the tribe's history and **traditions.** People can visit the reservation's museum and art gallery. The museum has a variety of traditional **artifacts,** including tools, musical instruments, clothing, and weapons. The reservation also has a re-creation of a traditional village. The Renape were once part of the great Powhatan **Confederacy,** which was centered along the Virginia coast.

THE RAMAPOUGH MOUNTAIN INDIANS

This group of New Jersey Indians incorporated in 1978 and are possibly **descendants** of the Munsee group of the Lenape. After the Lenape land was taken by white settlers, a small group of Munsees fled to the Ramapo Mountains. Because there were no roads or trails into the mountains, the white settlers paid very little attention to these Indians. Today, the Ramapough Mountain Indians have their headquarters in Mahwah, New Jersey, in Bergen County.

Lenape Influences

The influence of the Lenape can still be seen in much of New Jersey, especially in the names of its towns—from Hackensack to Hohokus to Piscataway. Every town that has a Lenape name has an English translation, and some are quite beautiful. Tuckahoe means "where the deer are shy," Cinnaminson means "sweet waters," and Pennsauken means "crooked river."

The American Indians in New Jersey today live in a world of technology, like everyone else. But many American Indians work to keep their **culture** and traditions alive and to share their heritage with other people who live in New Jersey. Through their efforts, we can gain a clearer understanding of our land, our history, and ourselves.

Map of New Jersey

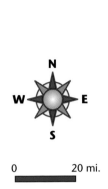

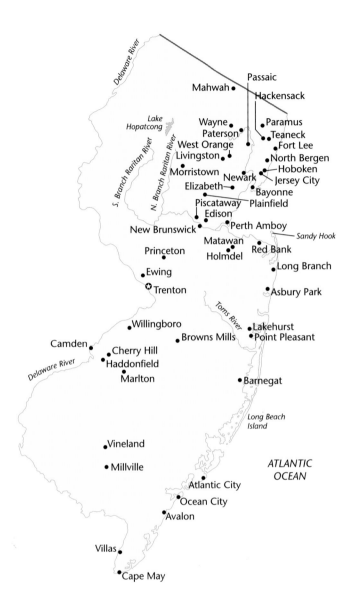

Timeline

ca. 10,000 B.C.E.	Paleo-Indians arrive in New Jersey and become the first people to live there.
1524 C.E.	Italian explorer Giovanni da Verrazano sails up the Atlantic coast past several Lenape settlements.
1609	Lenapes meet English sea captain Henry Hudson.
1620s	Dutch traders establish trading posts in Lenape territory.
1643	A group of Dutch soldiers **ambush** a Lenape camp in Pavonia, killing 80 people, including women and children. Indians of the region strike back by attacking Dutch settlers.
1650	The "Peach War" begins when a Dutchman kills a Lenape girl who was picking peaches on his property.
1655	The English take over the New Jersey colony from the Dutch.
1658	The Lenape are forced to take part in a treaty between the English and American Indian groups of the region. In following years, the Iroquois take Lenape land and claim authority over the Lenape people.
1700	Due to the effects of European diseases, only about 2,400 to 3,000 of the 12,000 original American Indians are left in the New Jersey colony.
1750s	By this time, the Lenape had lost all of their **traditional** lands.
1758	The New Jersey Assembly gives the remaining 200 or so Lenape a **reservation** that becomes known as Brotherton.
1802	Chief Lashar Tamar leads the last of the Brotherton Lenape to New Stockbridge, New York, to live with the Mahicans.
1832	The remaining New Jersey Lenape living with the Mahicans in New York resettle with American Indian groups west of the Mississippi River and in Canada.
1859	A group of Lenape settle in Anadarko, Oklahoma, which is now the only Lenape community recognized by the United States government.
1894	Indian Ann, the last full-blooded Lenape to live her entire life in New Jersey, dies.
2003	The State of New Jersey currently recognizes three American Indian tribes: the Nanticoke Lenni-Lenape Indians, Powhatan-Renape Nation, and Ramapough Mountain Indians.

Glossary

ambush make a surprise attack from a hidden place

American Revolution American war for independence from Great Britain that took place in 1775 through 1783

ancestor someone who came earlier in a family, especially earlier than a grandparent

archaeologist person who studies the lives of people in the past by examining the things they left behind

artifact object made by humans, such as a tool, pottery, or weapon

B.C.E. before the Common Era, also known as the Christian Era, which began with the birth of Jesus Christ

breechcloth small piece of clothing worn around the hips

ceremony special act or acts done on special occasions

Christianity religion that came from Jesus Christ and is based on the Bible; Eastern, Roman Catholic, and Protestant churches are Christian, as are members of those churches

confederacy group of peoples joined for some purpose

culture way of life of a group of people, including their food, clothing, shelter, and language

descendant person who comes from a particular ancestor or family

diplomat person whose work is keeping up relations between governments or groups of people

elaborate worked out with great care or detail

elder person who has authority because of age and experience

environment surrounding objects and conditions that affect living things

epidemic outbreak and rapid spread of disease to many people

extinct no longer living

fast go without food for a period of time

game animal animal that is hunted for food

glacier very large body of ice moving slowly over a wide area of land

gristmill mill for grinding grain

harpoon barbed spear used for hunting large fish

herb plant or part of plant used in medicine or in seasoning foods

heritage something handed down from the past or from one's ancestors

hominy kernels of corn with the outer shell, or hull, and germ removed

Ice Age period of time when a large part of the earth was covered with glaciers and the temperatures were cooler

immunity power to resist infection

incorporated joined or united into a single body

legislature body of people with the power to make, change, or cancel laws

measles contagious disease causing fever and red spots on the skin

medicine man important member of a tribe believed to have special healing powers and the ability to communicate with the spirits

migrate move from one region to another, or pass from one region to another on a regular schedule

mussel   shellfish with a soft body inside two shells hinged together

pelt   skin of an animal with its hair, wool, or fur

pension   sum paid regularly to a person who has retired from work

poverty   state of being poor

prehistoric   from the time before history was written

Presbyterian   member of a Presbyterian church. The Presbyterian Church is a Protestant Christian church with a system of representative governing bodies.

reservation   land set aside by the government for American Indians

ritual   established form for a ceremony or a system of rites

rugby   football game without time-outs, substitutions, interference, and forward passing; featuring kicking, dribbling, sideways and back passing, and tackling

sacred   holy, religious, or deserving respect and honor

shad   sea fishes related to herrings that have deep bodies, swim up rivers to spawn, and are important sources of food

sinew   tough band of tissue that connects muscles with bones

smallpox   very contagious and serious disease that causes a fever and sores on the skin

smoke   expose to smoke to give flavor and keep from spoiling; usually done with meat

spiritual   having a strong connection to the spirit or soul, apart from the body or material world; also having to do with religion

tradition   belief or custom handed down from one generation to another

upstate   mostly northerly and/or rural part of a state

wampum   beads made from shells and once used by American Indians for money or decoration

wigwam   dome-shaped American Indian home with a frame of poles covered with bark, rush mats, or animal hides

More Books to Read

Ansary, Mir Tamim. *Eastern Woodlands Indians.* Chicago: Heinemann Library, 2000.

Kraft, Herbert C. *The Lenape or Delaware Indians: The Original People of New Jersey, Southeastern New York State, Eastern Pennsylvania.* South Orange, N.J.: Seton Hall University Museum, 1996.

Lassieur, Allison. *The Delaware People.* Mankato, Minn.: Capstone Press, 2002.

Nardo, Don. *The Relocation of the Native American Indian.* Farmington Hills, Mich.: Kidhaven, 2001.

Wilker, Josh. *The Lenape Indians.* Broomall, Pa.: Chelsea House, 1993.

Index

About the Author

Mark Stewart makes his home in New Jersey. A graduate of Duke University with a degree in history, Stewart has authored more than 100 nonfiction titles for the school and library market. He and his wife Sarah have two daughters, Mariah and Rachel.